CH

D0623413

Being a great human being

is not related to gender,

it depends on caring about

the well-being of all our

fellow sentient beings.

Wu Yin

THE FEMALE BUDDHA

Discovering the
Heart of Liberation and Love

Deborah Bowman, Ph.D.

SAMADHI PUBLICATIONS

Boulder, Colorado

Reprinted from Chiyo-ni: Woman Haiku Master
by Donegan, Patricia and Ishebashi, Yoshi, Tokyo
Charles E. Tuttle Publishing, 1998.
Reprinted by permissi on of Patricia Donegan.

Reprinted from The First Buddhist Women: Translations
and Commentary on the Therigatha (1991)
by Susan Murcott with permission of Parallax Press,
Berkeley, California. www.parallax.org

Reprinted from Lotus Moon: The Poetry of Rengetsu (2005),
translation by John Stevens
with permission of White Pine Press
PO Box 236, Buffalo, NY 14201
www.whitepine.org

(c) Beata Grant, 2003. Reprinted from Daughters of Emptiness:
Poems of Chinese Buddhist Nuns
with permission from Wisdom Publications
199 Elm Street, Somerville, MA 02144 USA. www.wisdompubs.org

FIRST EDITION

Distributed in the United States by SAMADHI PUBLICATIONS

Library of Congress Control Number: 2011909182
Bowman, Deborah.
The Female Buddha: discovering the heart of liberation and love.—1st ed.
ISBN 978-098330590-3 hardcover

Printed in China
Through Bolton Associates
San Rafael, CA

Page 1
Wu Yin, *Choosing Simplicity: Commentary
on the Bhikshuni Pratimoksha,* NY: Snow
Lion Publications, 2001.

Page 2
Kwannon and Maple Leaves, Western Kyoto
cemetery, Japan

Page 3
Tara with Turquoise, Nalandabodhi Center,
Seattle, Washington, USA

Page 5
Guanyin and Sudhana, Jonli Temple,
Guanyin County, Taiwan

Page 7
Guanyin with Fire Halo, Lungshan Temple,
Taipei, Taiwan

Page 8
Quan Am holding a Mala, Ving Trang
Temple, My Tho, Vietnam

Page 10
Girls with Dharma Drum Lanterns, Lotus
Lantern Parade, Seoul, Korea

Page 13
Dharmachakra Mudra, Ocean Guanyin
Center, Keelung, Taiwan

Page 15
Woman with Chant Book, Jogyesa Temple,
Seoul, Korea

Page 16
Tara with Bow and Arrow, Tara Mandala
Retreat Center, Pagosa Springs, CO

CONTENTS

Foreword

Within every civilization there is a yearning for the feminine divine. We want to see our spiritual guides embodied not just in the iconic male representations but in female form. If I am to aspire to buddhahood, how much better it would be for my progress to have the model of a Buddha who shares the awareness and responses that I experience every day in my female body.

No matter how many times we are told that enlightenment transcends gender—and I'm sure it does—still we are left with all the gender differences and inequities that operate in our daily lives, whether we are men or women. And so we hunger to see femaleness mirrored in the figures that inspire us.

The Buddhist Celestial Bodhisattva of Compassion Kwan Yin in her beautiful manifestations as presented in the following pages is a hugely popular embodiment of the deity throughout Asia. And she has entered strongly into the West. Her acceptance into people's lives, with her message of bottomless compassion and her example of strength and resolve, derives no doubt from this great appetite among women and men for a female source of spiritual comfort and inspiration.

She hears our cries, she saves us from disaster, she may bring us children, she steers us toward compassionate acceptance of all that makes up a human being, and she models how to benefit others by acting from our own deepest nature.

I have been drawn to Kwan Yin for thirty years, researching her attributes and embodiments, writing about her, chanting to her, visualizing her. She presents endless insights and challenges to one who chooses to pay close attention to her.

Now I am so grateful to Deborah Bowman for gathering a wealth of images of this female Buddha, and for pairing them with the wisdom of our human sisters on the Buddhist path. Her informed and insightful introduction to this splendid book illuminates the significance of her photographs. For those who encounter Kwan Yin for the first time, as well as those of us who know her well, this book offers a rich, deep encounter with the female divine in all of us.

Sandy Boucher

Author of *Discovering Kwan Yin: Buddhist Goddess of Compassion*

Dream of Female Buddhas

TWENTY YEARS AGO I DREAMT I was walking in a large English garden in which there were three towering figures of female Buddhas carved out of stone. Each was over 100 feet tall sitting peacefully in meditation. In awe, I walked between them on quiet, carefully tended pathways. The wonder and serenity I felt in the presence of these majestic figures are indelible in my memory.

Coming at a time of great upheaval in my life, this dream was a spiritual landmark. Outwardly, I was counseling a large group of psychology students, trying to help them find a school in which they could complete their studies since their college was collapsing – it was about to close. Inwardly, I wrestled with the responsibility of leadership. Although I was no longer one of their teachers, I had willingly accepted the presidency of the college, a dying institution, in order to find a new home for their degree program. At the end of long days, overwhelmed by the loss of a community of learners, I often dissolved in tears of sadness.

Within weeks of this dream, I began conversations with a Buddhist-inspired college, The Naropa Institute. Interest on both sides quickly blossomed into planning sessions and within four months our displaced students were enrolling in a newly developed program that merged our transpersonal emphasis with comprehensive meditation and mindfulness practice. While I had previously studied and practiced Buddhism, over the course of my time at what is now Naropa University, I was led to make a personal commitment to the Buddhist path. Not only had the dream presaged my inner journey, it provided confirmation of the outer collaboration with Naropa as well.

On a deeper, archetypal level, I believe the female Buddhas reflect a progressive ripening of the consciousness of humankind. Dreams often show us what we are ignoring within ourselves, whether it is our potential, our wounds or our folly. As a psychologist, I have been witness to the profound impact of dreams of the Black Madonna on my clients and the tremendous love she represents to those who dream of her. From the Western Christian tradition, I believe she is an embodied image much like the female Buddhas in my dream.

The three figures in the garden came to me as feminine symbols representing the heart of Buddhist teachings. At the time of my distress I was not yet tapping into this gentle yet strong, resource of wisdom. It took their towering manifestation in my dream to rouse me to greater consciousness. Seventeen years later, in traveling through Asia, I discovered the female Buddha's ubiquitous presence in the form of Guanyin, a feminine icon of the enlightened heart and mind.

Spirit of Guanyin

IN 2007 I MET THE FEMALE BUDDHA on a trip to Vietnam with my husband, Stephen, who had first been there as a soldier. Now, forty years later, we were returning as Buddhists to visit where he was stationed, to heal memories of the Vietnam War, to practice at holy sites and to photograph Guanyin.

On our first day after our arrival we found Guanyin at every temple we visited in Cholon, the Chinese district of Ho Chi Minh City. As we continued our travels, my husband met former Vietnamese soldiers who empathetically swapped sorrowful stories of the war with him. It was healing to be met with the kindness of strangers. Quiet forest temples, with Guanyin welcoming us at the gates, were a balm and ancient reminder of a tradition that helped many people heal from the war.

As we visited temples in Vietnam, the head monk or nun would often go out of their way to greet us, offer tea and answer questions. Invariably a lay community member would interrupt with a pressing concern and our host would quickly go to find medical help for this person or resolve a dispute. The spirit of Guanyin was alive and well in a country of Engaged Buddhism, a term coined by Thich Nhat Hahn for social and environmental activism of the faith.

The following year I continued my search for Guanyin in Bangkok where the Chinese Diaspora was responsible for bringing her to Thailand. I presented papers there at conferences sponsored by the International Association of Buddhist Universities and looked for signs of the feminine on side trips to nearby places of worship. In traditional Thai temples, where only images of the historical Buddha grace the altars, this proved an intriguing challenge.

My first book, *The Luminous Buddha,* records some of these traditional images alongside quotes of Buddha's original teachings. This time, however, I was looking for something more elusive in a country where feminine representations are not overtly visible in temples, even though the feminine was clearly present in the gentle and gracious demeanor of the Thai people I met everywhere. My quest did not go unrewarded. Tucked away in the recesses of several temples, I would find tiny, and occasionally substantial, Guanyin statues adorned with fresh lotus buds and burning incense.

In 2009, I spent a week in Kyoto searching its many famous temples for images of Guanyin. Their figure of her, known as Kannon, is commonly depicted as either male or androgynous. Nevertheless a female version, referred to as Kwannon, surfaced unexpectedly for me when I stumbled on the eighty-foot memorial statue captured on the cover of this book. The veil draped over her head, typical of a female depiction, confirms her gender. For much of my time in Japan, I photographed the androgynous statues of Guanyin set in garden alcoves unrivaled for their stunning presentation in the landscape. Her presence was especially felt in the women who lined up to touch her statue at the exquisite Kiyomizu Temple, seeking blessings or a healthy childbirth.

This past year I stitched together a visit to Korea and Taiwan that was partially funded by Naropa. Timed during the Vesak celebrations of the Buddha's birth, enlightenment and passing away, I was able to visit Seoul for the Lotus Lantern Festival. My first day there, I was delighted to join hundreds of practitioners chanting under a canopy of colorful paper lanterns. On the evening of the Lotus Lantern parade, the culmination of Vesak celebrations, I witnessed thousands of joyful people carrying lighted paper lanterns down crowded streets of Seoul. At a mountain temple I discovered a large statue of Kuan Um, the Korean name for Guanyin, riding a water-spewing dragon. Her gentle guiding spirit seemed present as well in the women who held my hand and directed me to buses and subway trains on my way to pilgrimage sites.

In Taiwan, I reached the zenith of my overseas encounter

with Guanyin. A nun of the Luminary order, Jenkir Shih, was both my host and partner in the search for signs of the female Buddha. Tears came to my eyes when I met her female teacher, Master Wu Yin, and received guidance to sites where statues of Guanyin had significant spiritual meaning to the people of Taiwan. In the seasonable hazy weather, it was a challenge to get decent photographs, yet, inevitably, I found myself in locations where serendipitous opportunities allowed me to do just that. Lost on foggy Guanyin Mountain, said to be in the shape of her body, workers gave me a lift to a famous temple on its slopes where nuns were conducting a service in the last remaining light of the day.

In my final excursion, I had the honor of visiting nuns in Thailand and Myanmar. I met with Venerable Dhammananda who is making history in developing the first monastery for ordained nuns in Thailand. She is expanding the site her mother first established to offer trainings for women from around the world. In the Sagaing hills of Myanmar alone there are over 25,000 practicing women monastics. I had a delightful visit with a senior abbess who guides her nuns to continue their education up to the doctorate level.

A Crucial Transmission

THE LAST CENTURY HAS SEEN a steady transmission of Buddhism from East to West. Remarkable teachers came to Europe and the Americas and passed their lineages to the Western world. Translations enabled worldwide access to centuries of written words of wisdom. But an important dimension of the feminine face of Buddhism has yet to significantly impact the western audience. We've primarily been exposed to Asian male teachers, writers and masculine images of Buddhism, although the face of Buddhism in large parts of the East is also depicted as female.

In China and its considerable diaspora, no temple would be without a prominent statue of Guanyin. In Vietnam she is referred to as the female Buddha, something we discovered

in our travels when asking where to find temples with Quan Am, as she is known in Vietnam. Everyone who spoke even a little English would respond, "You mean the female

Buddha?" When a term such as "the female Buddha" enters the vernacular, the common language of a people, we can begin to understand her significance in the culture. Even in the United States, when I shared images of Guanyin from my travels with a Vietnamese-American, she remarked, "That's the lady Buddha!"

These encounters with the female Buddha in Vietnam inspired the title for this book. Continued travel, study and dialogue confirm that I am not alone in bringing the female Buddha forward. Lungshan Temple, the oldest Buddhist sanctuary in Taipei, is dedicated to Guanyin. She is the central figure on the main altar. In many of the countries I visited women practitioners far outnumbered the men I encountered in the temples. They serve not only as the primary body of volunteers but provide much of the material support for Buddhist activities. In Taiwan, nuns are the majority of monastics responsible for building religious, educational and medical facilities throughout the country.

Hearing the Cries of the World

IN INDIA, SEVERAL HUNDRED YEARS following the time of the Buddha, Guanyin began as male in the figure of Avalokiteshvara. His name means perceiver of sights, representing someone who could see and respond to all who cried out. When Buddhism came to China in the second century, Avalokiteshvara quickly developed as a central religious icon of compassion. He was said to offer succor to those in need and to answer the prayers of anyone who called out his name. By the eighth century, representations of Avelokiteshvara began appearing as female. In many legends she is characterized as *one who hears the cries of the world*, the translation of her Chinese name, Guanyin.

The female Guanyin is the most common visual presentation of Buddhism in parts of Asia. Her approachable image is more typically found in homes than a statue of the original Buddha. Large statues of Guanyin more often than not stand just within the entrance of temple grounds. Set in a garden alcove, the statue commonly has flowers, food and incense offered at her feet. Her connection to nature is emphasized by a willow branch she sometimes holds or an animal on which she may be sitting or standing. At ease on the back of a lion or dragon, she tames and utilizes powerful, instinctual energy. Her authority is equal to her kindness.

To many practitioners, Guanyin is a devotional image to which one offers prayers and makes requests. To others, she represents inner qualities of wisdom and loving-kindness. The outer image, a projection of our need for love and gentleness in the world, serves to calm our hearts and kindle faith. The inner image is a mirror of our essential, compassionate and enlightened mind.

The ultimate nature of mind is also the pure nature of the heart. Mind and heart are considered in their essence to be inseparable and without limit. Prabhas Dharma states, "When we are in a state of being Buddha, we are not reactive toward others, but always act from knowledge, realization and inner truth. Buddha is mind, free from conditioning." Guanyin, in the role of female Buddha, captures us with her unconditioned love and liberates our whole being, heart and mind.

Guanyin is distinguished by the Amitabha Buddha placed at the crown of her head. This manifestation represents the eternal Buddha and is said to signify the infinite light of the pure realm. In sculptures, Guanyin may be holding a sacred scroll or orb, symbol of the essence of the teachings. In China a cult formed around her "child granting" abilities and she is often seen holding an infant. This tradition still continues for men and women praying for a son to carry the family lineage. In this way Guanyin can be seen as assimilated to cultural values not necessarily aligned with core Buddhist teachings. While many of her depictions represent a gentle, maternal ideal, she is also sculpted in the fashion of the original Buddha, deep in meditation and unto herself.

The asexual ideal of the mother, expressed in the common form of Guanyin without breasts, matches a worldwide characterization of woman as saint versus woman as whore. Like the Virgin Mary in the Christian tradition, her elevation to goddess demands she be stripped of "dangerous" passions. But so are Jesus and Buddha. In these sexless depictions we observe the cultural preference towards an absolute ideal at the expense of our experience as physically embodied beings.

The legendary figure of Tara, a figure of compassion that is also considered a Buddha in the Tibetan lineage, is curvaceous and sexual. That is something suggested in only a few Chinese Guanyin legends where she offers liberation to men through sexual intercourse. Today we are beginning to see modern artistic expressions of her as a fully developed woman. Guanyin is growing up and so are we.

Buddhist nun Tenzin Palmo states, "I don't think that it matters whether the Buddha is male or female. He transcends both in my mind. But if it helps to think about female

Buddhas, that's fine." For myself, it helps to have a role model to which I can aspire. I thought my career options were limited to becoming a schoolteacher or a nurse. Who aspired to become a Buddha in the 50's? Where were the images of freedom and wisdom with which women could identify?

Women and men must learn to integrate positive feminine qualities as essential aspects of our enlightened nature. It is time for us to realize our unlimited potential in a multitude of colors, shapes and gender. We have very little time on this precious earth; like Guanyin, we must do whatever it takes to work for the liberation of humankind.

The Awakened Feminine

BRINGING FEMALE BUDDHIST IMAGES and teachers from East to West continues an essential transmission. Because of her sheer presence and veneration throughout eastern Asia, I've chosen Guanyin as the primary image of the female Buddha for this book. She is a wise, loving mother capable of relieving the pain of anyone who seeks her solace. Her enlightened heart guides her compassion. For these reasons and because she is an awakened being she is referred to as the female Buddha.

As a bodhisattva, Guanyin represents an aspiration for caring relationships, wisdom and service in the world. Through her tremendous efforts Guanyin is ready to attain Nirvana, the complete liberation from suffering. Yet she chooses to take the bodhisattva vow to forego this freedom until all beings are liberated from suffering as well. Having mastered the Buddhist teachings, she unceasingly shares her vast knowledge.

The female Buddha encourages men and women to perceive, accept and honor women's capacity for realization, seeing them as fully empowered and capable teachers of the tradition. She liberates all people to their full potential at a time when the planet needs as many enlightened beings as possible. As the Buddha in a woman's body, she brings the Buddhist teachings into the world through her benevolence and mercy. Zen Master

Daehaeng Sunim captures the essence of this feminine wisdom in her words, "If you do everything softly, everything can be solved." The female Buddha balances the many male images of the Buddha, helping us get beyond prescribed ideas of enlightenment limited to a masculine or feminine ideal.

Buddhist scholar Rita Gross states, "Even in some Buddhist cultures, which posit a very strong ethic of caring in the bodhisattva ideal, in practical, everyday ways, nurturing and caring for relationships are low priorities compared to practicing meditation and studying dharma texts." Her statement begs the question: Isn't selflessness, a quality to be realized through study and meditation, not put to the ultimate test in our ability to care for other beings? Is service not an equally essential training ground for enlightenment?

It is time to recognize compassionate ways of knowing often depicted as "feminine" as equal to wisdom ways of knowing typically typecast as masculine. Women and men need equal access to both. As stated by Buddhist author Sandy Boucher, "Wisdom needs compassion in order to soften its piercing insight; compassion needs wisdom to guide its expression."

An incorrect understanding of selflessness leads to painful behavior often assumed to be the proper role of women. Endless giving without renewal is not respectful of our basic goodness or Buddha Nature, which understands no self. No self means that we are not singular, independent or permanent. We don't exist as isolated entities because we are part of a fluid continuum of change. Our interdependence connects us to the vast web of life.

The female Buddha is not a model of martyrdom. Rather she represents strength in her knowledge of no self. Her giving is reciprocal with all phenomena. She cares for others as equal to herself. She cares for herself as equal to others. A symbol of contemplative practice and activity, the Female Buddha represents equal opportunity for men and women to awaken in this lifetime.

Dr. Myongsong Sunim, an often-quoted nun from Korea puts it this way, "I tell all the nuns that they must become awakened beings. By their own accomplishments they must become good knowing advisors. They must not kowtow anywhere they go. We must all become great women of the Way." It is time for all of us to stop scraping and bowing before doctrines and aspects of any tradition that denies our inherent greatness. Women in particular must work to overcome thousands of years of patriarchal thinking that limit our potential. Men must strive equally hard to see through their history of privilege in the religious sphere. We must all become the Buddha we were born to be, great human beings of peace and understanding. Angel Kyodo Williams reflecting on the

bodhisattva ideal states it succinctly, "We must leave no one behind."

Ground of Freedom

GUANYIN REPRESENTS A PARTICULAR EXPRESSION of Buddhism with many qualities associated to the feminine.

We can compare the most common depictions of her to Shakyamuni Buddha, the Buddha who walked this earth over 2500 years ago. Observable traits that respectively demonstrate feminine and masculine stereotypes are assigned to each one.

Guanyin is most commonly seen standing, holding a vase of healing fluids in one hand and with the other hand in a teaching mudra or gesture. The Buddha is most commonly represented seated in meditation, with one hand in a gesture of contemplation and the other in a teaching mudra. He may also be portrayed gesturing with other symbolic mudras while standing, walking or lying down. Guanyin may also be portrayed sitting in meditation or holding other sacred objects. While there is much convergence in these traditional images, it is through observing their divergent qualities that we come to understand Guanyin as a symbol of feminine presence.

Her standing posture implies doing; his sitting posture implies being. She appears relationally oriented; his posture emphasizes an interior point of reference. Depicted in meditation posture, his realization is generally characterized as the result of his solitary efforts. Her realization appears in a relational context. Her strength is soft; his appears concentrated. Both are enduring.

The Buddha epitomizes the seeker. Guanyin is the ideal of the mother. In his primary role of teacher he offers freedom while she offers refuge in her primary role as healer. She holds a vase offering a balm for the suffering of the world. He is empty-handed demonstrating that cessation of suffering requires nothing beyond ourselves. Each figure models distinct yet equal and complementary traits on the path of awakening.

While we must do the work ourselves, we always do it in the context of others. Our teaching heals and our healing teaches. Being and doing are not opposites but flow out of each other. Each requires concentrated, independent effort as well as vulnerability and openness to our environment. We seek refuge in the Buddha and are liberated by Guanyin. The mother births the seeker and the seeker realizes emptiness, a quality of impermanence and infinite openness symbolically depicted by Prajna Paramita, the Mother of the Buddhas.

As a seeker, the Buddha achieved realization and then spent the next forty-five years in the role of a Buddha and a bodhisattva. He taught the path to liberation and freedom from suffering. Teaching in order to liberate others is often considered the highest calling of a bodhisattva. Guanyin, on the other hand, is a mythological bodhisattva. She serves with a thousand eyes and a thousand arms, offering freedom through any means possible. She is a shape-changer who becomes a Buddha if necessary to free a particular being. She teaches by doing whatever it takes to alleviate suffering and bring human beings to awakening. Through her own realization she provides the ground of freedom for others. Not representing any one woman, she may be said to symbolize the accumulated history of innumerable selfless acts of women, loving unconditionally throughout time and space.

A Shifting Paradigm

IN HER BOOK, *WOMEN IN BUDDHISM* Scholar Diane Paul points out the broad spectrum of attitudes toward women embedded in sutras written as words of the Buddhist faith. In the most misogynist texts, women are castigated as evil temptresses and morally weak. Other sutras show women as aspiring on the Buddhist path although they must be reborn as men to achieve enlightenment as bodhisattvas or Buddhas. In *The Sutra of Queen Srimala of the Lion's Roar,* Queen Srimala has reached the highest stage on the bodhisattva path to be reborn in her next life as a Buddha. Verses describe Queen Srimala's father as Shakyamuni Buddha and her mother as Amitabha Buddha who inhabits the Pure Land, a place beyond suffering. The *Lion's Roar* speaks to the transitory nature of truth, that all forms are mere appearances that rise and fall away.

Guanyin represents a pull to balance our tendency to value absolute truth over relative truth, or what we judge as mundane. Guanyin helps us see the sacred in our wholeness as she stands for the unconditional love of a mother for her child. She is without projection and sees only our pure Buddha Nature, which cannot be tarnished by the world. When she hears our cries, her empathy penetrates our isolation and self-judgment, completely freeing all obstructions to healing. Symbolically she balances the objective sky-father qualities of the male Buddha, emblematic of absolute truth, with her grounded, earth-mother energy.

In celebrating an image of the female Buddha we challenge the old myth with a new myth. We play with form to shake up habitual thinking and honor diverse paths to Buddha-hood. For many centuries, artists have been playing with this edge, expressing Guanyin in Buddha postures in sculpture and painting.

Could it be our collective imagination is holding Guanyin as both bodhisattva and Buddha? This new myth mirrors expanding awareness about the capacity for women to not only gain enlightenment, but to lead the way to liberation. The female Buddha points to a shifting paradigm beyond prejudice, asking us to step forward and bring freedom to all.

Compassionate Action

INCLUDED IN THIS BOOK ARE THREE bodhisattva figures often associated with Guanyin: Tara as she developed in the Tibetan Buddhist tradition, Mazu associated in China with both Taoism and Buddhism, and Jizo Bodhisattva as he developed in Japan.

Born of a tear from the eye of Avelokiteshvara, Tara is venerated as an emanation of his compassion and is also considered a Buddha. Her many deified forms are utilized in spiritual practices for gaining enlightenment through embodying her essence. Guanyin Scholar Chun-Fang Yu suggests that her maternal manifestation as White Tara may be a source of influence in the development of the white-robed Guanyin in China. Both are considered "mothers of mercy" in offering physical healing and serenity of mind. Like Guanyin, the energized manifestation of Green Tara offers protection in the world and represents awakened activity. Guanyin and Tara are also both closely related to the eternal Buddha, Amitabha, each wearing an image of him at the top of their heads.

The Chinese figure Mazu, also known as the Queen Mother or the Empress of Heaven, is intimately connected with Guanyin at sites of worship. She is considered in legends to be an emanation of Guanyin, since her birth came about when her parents prayed to Guanyin for a child. As a child, Mazu also prayed to Guanyin to assist her parents. There are stories that suggest a drop of their blood co-mingled and Guanyin is the mother or sister of Mazu. Both are maternal figures and protectors of those in danger. In coastal areas Mazu was believed to save sailors at sea and many temples in her honor were built at sites where ships from China first landed safely. It is common to find Buddhist and Taoist practitioners at temples where both Guanyin and Mazu reside.

Jizo and Kannon, as Guanyin is known in Japan, are often venerated together as a sacred pair embodying compassion and protecting the innocent. Holding an infant, Jizo escorts children who have died to the heavenly abode of the Pure Land. His statue is sought to console those who have lost children or who suffer from illness. Like Guanyin, Jizo, whose name translates as Earth Treasury or Earth Womb, is grounded in helping others.

Words and Images

THE QUOTATIONS IN THIS BOOK REPRESENT a fusion of many schools of Buddhist teachings and women teachers from around the world. The quotes are by women from the time of the Buddha to the present and many represent three of the main schools of Buddhism – Theravada, Mahayana and Vajrayana. Theravada is the oldest school aligned to the

original teachings of the Buddha. The Mahayana approach, including Pure Land Buddhism, developed later and includes many sutras emphasizing the path of the Bodhisattva. The Vajrayana developed in Tibet and incorporates teachings from the previous two schools plus further expansion on the nature of emptiness and paths to its realization. While the female version of Guanyin evolved out of the Mahayana tradition, all three traditions express the wisdom her image reflects.

The exceptional women quoted in this book are teachers, authors and spiritual leaders from around the world. Most are lineage holders in each of the three major Buddhist traditions, including nineteen ordained nuns. Several of these nuns are considered accomplished masters. Numerous quotations from the West are by senior teachers and by women who have been ordained as priests. One highly regarded lay teacher, Upasika Kee Nanayon, is a woman who arose to veneration in the unlikely soil of male dominated Thai Buddhism.

Many passages are from women who are professors, writers and poets widely recognized for their scholarship, insight and creativity. Aung San Suu Kyi, quoted as a Nobel Peace

Laureate, was elected Prime Minister of Burma in 1990 and immediately put under house arrest where she remained for 15 of the last 20 years, inspired by Buddhist practice and principles of nonviolence. Recently released, she is considered a living bodhisattva in her country.

The nuns who spoke over 2500 years ago are the first recorded voices of women in religious history. They put their experience into poems of enlightenment, many contrasting their excruciating experience as the property of men in their former roles as wives or prostitutes. Missing from this collection are the never recorded voices of thousands of highly adept female practitioners as well as an incalculable number of women silenced by a history of entrenched patriarchy. Also not heard are the written words of many more accomplished women teachers who could not fit into this small book. I can only hope to quote their wise words in a second volume.

A Common Chord

While researching the teachings of women from around the world, I have been immersed in their profound experiences and reflections. I encourage you to seek the gifts they offer in their many books of immense insight.

Alongside each image you will find information about the setting of each photograph. Representing several major countries of the diaspora of India, China and Tibet, the pictures are from Vietnam, Taiwan, Korea, Japan, Thailand, Cambodia, Myanmar and the United States. I've taken the creative liberty of juxtaposing the wisdom of an African-American Zen priest with a photograph of a Korean nun playing cymbals in a parade. The truths are universal whether expressed in words or a serene face.

The Female Buddha celebrates the fullness of life and our capacity to see through compassionate eyes of non-discriminating awareness, the eyes of a Buddha. She embodies awakened feminine qualities that live in both women and men. Reminding us of our full human birthright, she is gentle and strong, compassionate and free. My hope is *The Female Buddha* will touch seekers of all faiths and curiosity, striking a common chord in the heart of humanity.

Notes

The spelling of Guanyin in this text is in the Pinyin style. Pinyin is now considered the standard for Chinese Mandarin in Mainland China and Taiwan. Kwan Yin and Quan Yin are considered Cantonese spellings derived from Hong Kong and Southern parts of China and are also in common usage in the West.

Deborah Bowman, *The Luminous Buddha: Image and Word,* (Blurb, Inc., 2007).

Prabhas Dharma, in Karma Lekshe Tsomo, ed. *Buddhism Through American Women's Eyes* (Ithaca, NY: Snow Lion Publications, 1995), 29.

Tenzin Palmo, *Reflections on a Mountain Lake* (NY: Snow Lion Publications, 2002), 83.

Daehaeng Sunim, "Who is Healing" in Martine Bachelor, *Walking on Lotus Flowers,* (London: Thorsons, 1996), 171.

Rita Gross "Where are the Women in the Refuge Tree: Teacher, Student, and Gender in Buddhism" in Rita Gross and Rosemary Radford Ruether, Religious Feminism and the Future of the Planet: a Buddhist-Christian Conversation (NY: Continuum: 2001), 74.

Sandy Boucher, *Opening the Lotus: A Woman's Guide to Buddhism* (Boston: Beacon Press, 1997), 127.

Myongsong Sunim, "The Water and the Wave," in Martine Bachelor, ed. *Walking on Lotus Flowers* (London: Thorsons, 1996), 81.

Angel Kyodo Williams, Being Black: *Zen and the Art of Living with Fearlessness and Grace* (NY: Viking Compass, 2000), 100.

Diane Paul, *Women in Buddhism: Images of the Feminine in Mahayana Tradition* (Berkeley: Asian Humanities Press, 1979).

Chun-fang Yu, *Kuan-yin: The Chinese Transformation of Avalokitesvara* (NY: Columbia University Press, 2001), 250. Dr. Yu states, "The White-robed Kuan-yin might be derived from the Tantric sutras, but the actual creation of the iconography was entirely an indigenous one." Her scholarship points to the influence of White Tara from the Tantric tradition on the development of Guanyin yet sees the transformation of Avelokitesvara to the female Guanyin as a completely Chinese phenomenon.

Turning the Pages, Walking the Path

Welcome to inspiration from
the Female Buddha. She is your
essential nature.

Contemplate the following pages
slowly. Let the words and images
pour over you.

Reflect on a passage once each week
or randomly open the book
when you need a mindful gap.

Relax and enjoy.

Temple Steps | Arashiyama district, Kyoto, Japan. These lovely steps lead to a temple in the hills just west of Kyoto. This temple was closed for the day and I could not find an English sign translating its name. Wandering in the neighboring area I could not place it on my tourist map nor ignore a sense of bliss in the moss covered forest.

Breathe, pay attention to what's in front of you, what's being offered.

China Galland

Woman Stringing Flowers and Tray of Roses | Flower Market, Bangkok, Thailand. Searching for images of Guanyin in the Chinese district of Bangkok, I was lost more often than not. Surrendering to the lively scene of the nearby Flower Market, I was delighted to see signs of the Bodhisattva everywhere. Women strung garlands for Buddhist offerings, not only as a livelihood, but also with devotion and a generous heart.

China Galland, *Longing for Darkness*, London: Arkana, 1990. Galland is a professor-in-residence at the Center for the Arts, Religion and Education at the Graduate Theological Union in California, where she directs the Keepers of Love project. She has won awards for fiction and nonfiction.

People often find it difficult even to form an idea of inner joy, much less experience it. We need to accept the fact it exists within us and that we can discover it.

Ayya Khema

Three Smiling Boddhisattvas | Tom Son Hoi Quan Pagoda, Ho Chi Minh City. These three cheerful, blue-haired Guanyin figures made me smile on a hot, sweaty day of sleuthing for images of the saint in the Chinese district. The left-facing svastika (Sanskrit) on their chest is a common symbol in Buddhism for an auspicious object or place. It is not to be confused with the later use of the right-facing swastika in Nazi Germany.

Ayya Khema, *When the Iron Eagle Flies: Buddhism for the West*, London: Arkana: 1991. Ayya Khema escaped Nazi Germany as a child and became a nun in the Theravadin tradition in Sri Lanka where she later developed a center for training nuns. She wrote 25 books on meditation and Buddhism.

To be with oneself in meditation, either alone or in the company of others, is a symbol of reclaiming power and utilizing the power of our inner resources of attention and sensitivity to nurture our freedom.

Christina Feldman

White Marble Guanyin | Wat Indravihan, Bangkok, Thailand. The vase Guanyin holds may be traced back in history to earlier Brahman figures in India using a water flask in cleansing rituals. The two small figures on the altar with Guanyin represent her Chinese inspired attendants, the Dragon Maiden and Sudhana, also known as Virtuous Wealth. One is carrying a jewel representing the enlightened teachings.

Christina Feldman, *Woman Awake*, London: Arkana, 1990. Feldman studied meditation in Asia and has been leading Insight Meditation retreats since 1974. She co-founded the Gaia House for Insight Meditation in England and teaches regularly in the U.S. and Europe.

While sometimes I feel extremely vulnerable,
Kwan Yin lets me realize that my only safety
lies in the emergence of the tenderest part
of myself, to meet the needs of each moment.

Sandy Boucher

Mother and Daughter Offerings | Wat Phra Kaeo, Bangkok. These two women offer lotus blossoms, incense and candles at an altar to Guanyin within the Royal Palace complex in Bangkok. The presence of Guanyin figures at sites in Thailand is seen in large cities where Chinese practitioners also come to visit. Guanyin is becoming an important figure for a growing number of Thai women.

Sandy Boucher, *Discovering Kwan Yin, Buddhist Goddess of Compassion*, Beacon Press: Boston, Mass., 1999. Boucher introduces Buddhism to women in numerous books and articles on women's spirituality. Her vivid and personal writing on Kwan Yin tells us how to bring her gifts of compassion into our contemporary lives.

Our practice must be careful, meticulous, patient.
We must face everything.

Charlotte Joko Beck

Daibenkudokuten, Sanjusangen-do, Kyoto, Japan | This female bodhisattva of compassion is a life size wood sculpture made in the eighteenth century. Equated to Sri Devi Laksmi of the Hindu tradition, Daibenkudokuten is born of the sea and symbolizes prosperity. She stands in front of a thousand carved figures from the eleventh century of Kannon (Guanyin).

Charlotte Joko Beck, *Nothing Special*, Harper: San Francisco, 1993. Beck, a western teacher trained in the Zen tradition, shared penetrating insight while guiding her students in working with body awareness and emotions. Her first book, *Everyday Zen,* became an underground best seller.

An awareness of the immanence of death imbues
life with greater intensity and meaning.

Karma Lakshe Tsomo

Work Practice | Songdhammakayani Monastery, Thailand. In the long shadows of dusk these nuns finish their afternoon chores raking the monastic grounds. For these women the day begins and ends with formal meditation yet all aspects of their daily activities is considered an opportunity for mindfulness practice.

Karma Lekshe Tsomo, *Into the Jaws of Yama, Lord of Death: Buddhism, Bioethics, and Death*, NY: State University of New York Press: 2006. Karma Lekshe Tsomo is an Associate Professor of Theology and Religious Studies at the University of San Diego. She is the editor of numerous books compiling the wisdom of women Buddhist teachers from around the world.

Practicing compassionate acceptance
is like being in love
and seeing the face of the beloved
in every moment
as if for the first time.

Cheri Huber

Guanyin figurine on Temple Roof | Wat Chaleom Phra Kiet, Nonthaburi, Thailand
The large rambling grounds of this temple on the northern outskirts of Bangkok had numerous large and small statues of
the Buddha. I found this tiny porcelain figure of Guanyin incorporated into a mosaic flourish on the roof of one of the
buildings. Used prolifically in Thai art, mosaic was originally brought to the country from China.

Cheri Huber, *When You're Falling, Dive*, CA: Keep it Simple Books, 2003. Huber is founder and resident teacher of
the Zen Monastery Peace Center and the Mountain View Zen Center, both in California. Her books address topics
including depression, fear, teens, parents, psychology and meditation.

Although I'm thin and weak
Spring in my once lively gait gone – gone –
I've climbed the mountain
leaning on my walking stick
I throw the cloak off my shoulder
Overturn the little begging bowl
Against this rock I lean
and prop the self of me
Break through the gloom
that boxed me in *Ahhhhh*

Citta

Elderly Woman at Temple Gate | Quan Cong Hoi Temple, Can Tho, Vietnam
This woman graciously returned our smile as she sat just inside a quiet temple courtyard in the center of the busy city of Can Tho. Despite rapid economic development in Vietnam, most elderly are still cared for by their families. A small but growing percent of the elderly, particularly widowed women, are without financial support.

Citta, Andrew Schelling and Anne Waldman, *Sons and Daughters of the Buddha*, Shambhala Publications: Boston, Mass, 1996. Citta was a wealthy woman who became a renunciate nun in India at the time of the Buddha. Her poems are recorded in the Therigatha. She gained great insight in old age while sitting at a place where the Buddha taught.

Evening temple bell
stopped in the sky
by cherry blossoms

Chiyo-ni

Bronze Praying Girl | Chion-in Pagoda, Kyoto, Japan
This lovely statue of a young girl is at the entrance to a thirteenth century Pure Land Buddhist temple. She holds her hands in gassho, a mudra of reverence. She kneels to offer respect and humility. Visitors place coins in the folds of her robes. Chion-in Pagoda was the original temple of Rengetsu, a poet nun quoted in this book.

Donegan, Patricia and Ishebashi, Yoshi, *Chiyo-ni: Woman Haiku Master,* Tokyo: Charles E. Tuttle Publishing, 1998. Chiyo-ni, a disciple of the poet Basho in the 18th century, is widely regarded as one of the great haiku poets. She became a Buddhist nun as a way "to teach her heart to be like the clear water, which flows night and day."

To commit to love is fundamentally to commit to a life beyond dualism. That's why, in a culture of domination love is so sacred. It erodes dualisms— the binary oppositions of black and white, male and female, right and wrong. Love transforms.

bell hooks

Bikkhuni and dog | Songdhammakayani Monastery, Thailand. This sweet moment between a nun and a dog cared for by the monastery came after her full day of practice, study and work in the garden. I was taken by the gentle and profound demeanor of the sisters practicing under Venerable Dhammananda, the abbess of the only monastery for women in Thailand.

bell hooks, *Contemplation and Transformation*, in Marianne Dresser, ed., Buddhist Women on the Edge, Berkeley, CA: North Atlantic Books, 1996. hooks is a distinguished Professor at the City College in New York and the author of many books on topics including racism, feminism and memoir. Her wise sensibility shines through her essays on Buddhism.

We are all human beings. We all wish to have happiness and to avoid suffering. Take the time to imagine yourself in another's shoes. Count your blessings. Try as much as possible to practice loving kindness. At the very least, try to avoid harming others.

Jan Willis

Nun Conducting Service | Lingyun Zen Temple, Guanyinshan, Taiwan
This large Avelokitesvara figure dominates the central worship hall. The nun strikes the large gong to emphasize significant phrases in the evening chants. At the end of the service another nun strikes a tremendous drum hanging from the ceiling and then a massive bell on the other side of the temple. The thunderous tones struck deep in my being.

Jan Willis, *Dreaming Me: Black, Baptist and Buddhist,* NY: Riverhead Books, 2001. Willis is a Professor of Religion at Wesleyan University where she has taught since 1977. She studied in India and is a dynamic writer and speaker on issues of race, feminism and Buddhism.

Pregnant Woman touching Kannon | Kiyomizu Temple, Kyoto, Japan
Touching this statue of Avelokitesvara is said to bring blessings and good luck to pregnant women and the children
they are carrying. In China, only female deities had child-granting capacities and Guanyin took on this role. She is also
considered the patron saint of mothers.

Woman touching Kannon | Kiyomizu Temple, Kyoto, Japan
Women line up to touch this bronze Guanyin statue at this large temple complex. The ambiance at this outdoor site
was ebullient and serene, the silence punctuated with laughter lilting through the air. The particular Indian motif of this
sculpture was distinctive in comparison with most of the Kannon statues I saw in Japan.

Judith L. Lief, *Making Friends with Death: A Buddhist Guide to Encountering Mortality*, Boston: Shambhala, 2001.
Acharya Lief is a senior teacher in the Tibetan Buddhist and Shambhala traditions. She is a pastoral counselor and teaches
on death and dying and the application of mindfulness-awareness training.

When we give and receive, giver and receiver are on equal ground. One is not higher or lower than the other. Generosity is an exchange, not a one-way street. Generosity connects us with each other, whether we are the giver or the receiver, and enriches us both.

Judith Lief

When our mind is embued with compassion, we don't view others as enemies or obstacles to our happiness. Instead, we see that they do harmful actions because they wish to be happy but don't know the correct method of attaining happiness. They are, in fact, just like us: imperfect, limited sentient beings who want happiness and not suffering. Thus, we can accept them as they are and seek to benefit them in the future.

Thubton Chödrön

Mary, Quan Am and St. Ann | Marble Mountain, Vietnam

Statues of Mary and Guanyin are ubiquitous in Vietnam. When I showed this photo on the back of my camera to a Buddhist nun I met, she pointed to each of the three figures and said, "Guanyin, Guanyin, Guanyin—all Mother." In that moment I experienced delight, as she alluded to the reverence for the Loving Mother that is shared across world wisdom traditions.

Thubton Chödrön, *Taming the Mind,* NY: Snow Lion Publications, 2004. An American-born Tibetan nun, Thubton Chödrön studied in India and Nepal. She leads the Sravasti Abbey, a monastic community in Washington State. She emphasizes the practical application of Buddha's teachings in our lives.

Every day, at the moment when things get edgy
we can just ask ourselves, "Am I going to practice
peace, or am I going to war?"

Pema Chödrön

Woman Lighting Incense | Quan Am Pagoda, Ho Chi Minh City, Vietnam
The air was full of burning incense as women and men lit incense before making offerings at the many altars and large stone or copper urns. This woman, one of many, was intent with her prayers at this pagoda dedicated to Quan Am (Guanyin) and Mazu, the Celestial Holy Mother in the Chinese pantheon of deities.

Pema Chödrön, *When Things Fall Apart: Heart Advice for Difficult Times.* Shambhala: Boston, 1997. Pema Chödrön is an American Buddhist nun and author of many books with compelling titles such as *Start Where You Are* and *The Wisdom of No Escape.* She is the resident teacher at Gampo Abbey, a monastery in Nova Scotia.

We should do what we believe is right, even if one is afraid. Of course, we cannot help being afraid; we just have to work to control our fear.

Aung San Suu Kyi

Teaching Mudra | Vietnamese Pagoda, Bangkok, Thailand
Guanyin's hand gesture joins two fingers, representing bringing together wisdom and skillful means. When the figure of Guanyin displays this Dharmachakra, or teaching mudra, we are reminded of the depth of her mission, to bring all beings into freedom by uniting the wisdom of clear seeing with compassionate action.

Hand and Vase | Vietnamese Pagoda, Bangkok, Thailand
In the teaching mudra, the hand is held in front of the heart, symbolizing that Guanyin's teachings emanate straight from the heart. The vase held just beneath the other hand demonstrates the direct relationship between the Buddhist teachings and the healing nectar that flows from her sacred container.

Aung San Suu Kyi, *Freedom From Fear: And Other Writings,* London: Penguin Books, 1991. p.219. Aung San Suu Kyi, recently freed from house detention in Burma, continues to work for democracy and the freedom of her people. She has become an international symbol of peaceful resistance in the face of political oppression.

Paper Dragon Float | Lotus Lantern Parade, Seoul, Korea
Children chased after this dragon, then screamed and laughed when it breathed fire into the night air. Almost sixty feet long, it snaked its way down a crowded central avenue in the heart of Seoul. In Asia, the dragon is a cherished symbol of powerful forces for goodwill and fortunate circumstances.

Riding the Dragon | Doseon-sa Temple, Korea
Her demeanor calm, Guanyin rides the back of this water-spewing dragon with quiet dignity. The Dragon, Water, the Mother and Guanyin all represent yin, the feminine element associated with the void, from which all life emerges. The receptive energy of yin and the dynamic, masculine energy of yang are considered equal and complementary.

Tsultrim Allione, *Feeding Your Demons: Ancient Wisdom for Resolving Inner Conflict,* NY: Little, Brown and Company, 2008. Lama Tsultrim Allione was ordained a Tibetan nun in 1970 and later returned her vows to marry and raise a family. She is author of *Women of Wisdom* and founder of Tara Mandala Retreat Center in Colorado.

Normally we empower our demons by believing they are real and strong in themselves and have the power to destroy us. As we fight against them, they get stronger. But when we acknowledge them by discovering what they really need, and nurture them, our demons release their hold, and we find that they actually do not have power over us.

Tsultrim Allione

Only the wounded healer is able to heal. As long as we think that spiritual leaders need to be perfect, we live in poverty. I have perfect teacher inside; there is no perfect teacher outside.

Sandra Jishu Holmes

Woman polishing a Buddha | Marble Street in Mandalay, Myanmar
Creating Buddha statues is an act of devotion as well as a livelihood for the women and men working on the many neighborhood blocks of Marble Street. With great concentration this woman is putting the final touches on a statue before a blessing is offered.

Sandra Jishu Holmes, Angel Kyodo Williams, *Being Black: Zen and the Art of Living with Fearlessness and Grace,* NY: Viking Compass, 2000. Roshi Holmes co-founded the Buddhist inspired Greyston Mandala in New York, a center dedicated to improving the lives of homeless families, single mothers and poor people living with HIV/AIDS. She died in 1998.

Approach what you find repulsive, help the ones you think you cannot help, and go to the places that scare you.

Machig Lobdron

Cave Altar | Marble Mountain, Vietnam
These small figurines and burning incense sticks are left by pilgrims visiting the shrines and historical pagodas built within the caves of Marble Mountain in central Vietnam. The visitors offer incense and flowers at every Guanyin and Buddha statue. The tradition of stone carving in this area spans seven centuries to the present day.

Machig Lobdron, Chödrön, Pema, *When Things Fall Apart,* Shambhala: Boston, 1997. Machig Lobdron, both an historical and mythologized figure, was born in Tibet in the 11th century. Recognized as a great lama during her life, her teachings draw on the inspiration of texts of the Mother of Perfection Wisdom.

By the power of my
earnest aspiration,
may I bring peace
to innumerable and
unlimited living beings.

Queen Srimala

Mazu, Empress of Heaven | Kheng Hock Keong temple, Yangon, Myanmar. Mazu is the central figure in the main altar of this Chinese temple where many women practitioners were offering prayers. In China Mazu was elevated to royal status during a dynasty intent on expanding its influence through spiritual icons. She is also well known as the protector of sailors and the Queen Mother.

Head Abbess | Samaidodaya Recluse, Sagaing, Myanmar
At eighty-nine years of age Daw Ku La Pa Ti is the head abbess of a monastery of 250 nuns. She told us about the preceding three generations of abbesses, all living over ninety years of age. The Sagaing hills are the home of over 25,000 practicing nuns.

Srimala, Diana Y. Paul, *The Sutra of Queen Srimala of the Lion's Roar,* CA: Bukkyo Dendo Kyokai and Numata Center for Buddhist Translation and Research, 2004. In the Indian tradition, Queen Srimala is a lay bodhisattva who possesses the "lions roar" of great eloquence. In the third century she is said to have delivered the profound teachings conveyed in the sutra that is named after her.

The very part that we don't recognize in ourselves is the part that will give us trouble. Our practice is to become wider and bigger, to encompass more energies, more ways of living, more images. Whenever we see ourselves resisting, angry, unhappy, there's the place to go. There's the bowing mat.

Jan Chozen Bays

Prostration | Jogyesa Temple, Seoul, Korea
The posture of prostration is common across religions, reminding the practitioner of an attitude of humility, respect and supplication. In Buddhism, this deep bow is an offering of one's total commitment to the path and a willingness to let go of everything. It is also an opportunity to pay homage to a teacher and purify obscurations to enlightenment.

Jan Chozen Bays "Taking Realization into Everyday Life" in Ellen S. Sidor, *A Gathering of Spirit: Women Teaching in American Buddhism, Rhode Island*: Primary Point Press, 1987. Sensei Bays is a pediatrician, Zen teacher and author of *Jizo Bodhisattva: Guardian of Children, Travelers, and Other Voyagers*. She shares healing stories of Jizo and her experience as a physician.

The state in which my inner mind is not grasping, not excited, not busy, is a state where my mind has settled down completely, in the same way as the water settles down. The sea of the mind, the deep water of the mind, when it settles quietly, this is concentration.

Myongsong Sunim

Blackened Bronze Guanyin | Wat Phra Kaew, Bangkok, Thailand
Prominently placed at the Royal Palace in Bangkok, this female statue speaks to the large influence of the Chinese Mahayana diaspora in Thailand. Today, individuals from both the Theravada and Mahayana traditions can be seen making offerings to Guanyin as a figure of compassion.

Myongsong Sunim, "The Water and the Wave" in Martine Bachelor, Walking on Lotus Flowers, London: Thorsons, 1996. Myongsong Sunim is President of the National Bhikkhuni assembly of the Korean Buddhist Jogye Order and Dean of the Graduate School, Un Mun Sangha College. She is an advocate for the ordination of Buddhist nuns worldwide.

Guanyin and Parrot | Phouc An Hoc Quan Pagoda, Ho Chi Minh City, Vietnam
Carrying Guanyin's beads, the parrot flying next to Guanyin vowed to forever accompany her after she relieved him of consuming grief after the death of his mother. He has become a symbol of filial piety, an attitude of deep respect towards one's parents and ancestors. In most depictions the parrot is white and in a few tales the parrot represents Guanyin's loyal husband.

White-robed Guanyin | Phouc An Hoc Quan Pagoda, Ho Chi Minh City, Vietnam
Guanyin protects the entrance of this temple in Cholon, the Chinese district of Ho Chi Minh City. Wearing white, she signifies the enlightened mind. The white-robed Guanyin is also known to help women conceive and represents her maternal instincts.

Anne Caroline Klein, *Meeting the Great Bliss Queen: Buddhists, Feminists and the Art of the Self,* Boston: Beacon Press, 1995. Klein is Professor and Chair of Religious Studies at Rice University. She is the co-founder of Dawn Mountain Tibetan Temple in Texas and has done extensive field work in Asia.

...the womb of enlightenment is possessed by all living things, and its fruit depends above all on oneself, not on another, not even Buddha. It is therefore within the province of any person to reap from her own Buddha-womb her own Buddhahood.

Anne Carolyn Klein

Woman with Bindi | Lotus Lantern Parade, Seoul, Korea
Buddhists, as well as Hindus, are sometimes known to wear a Bindi, the red dot on the forehead, as a symbol of wisdom and concentration. Marching in the parade, this woman's spirit of joy was infectious. Each lay or monastic group in the parade wore particular colors and carried paper lanterns in the shape of a Buddhist symbol.

Making a Lotus Lantern | Lotus Lantern Street Festival, Seoul, Korea
Daytime activities of the festival included opportunities for children and adults to make a lantern or color in an image of Guanyin. Tables were set up for foreigners with interpreters ready to explain the celebratory tradition or how to make a lotus lantern.

Maura O'Halloran *Pure Heart, Enlightened Mind: the Zen Journal and Letters of Maura "Soshin" O'Halloran,* NY: Riverhead Books, 1994. O'Halloran studied in Japan, was ordained a nun and became a Zen teacher. Returning to Ireland to teach, she died at 27 in an accident in Thailand. She is venerated as a saint at the temple she practiced at in Japan.

Not that I expect to change the world or even a blade of grass, but it's as if to give myself is all I can do, as the flowers have no choice but to blossom.

The nature of the mind, the Buddha nature, is not my Buddha-nature or her Buddha-nature. It's just Buddha-nature. It's like the sky. It's infinite and all-encompassing. It's what we all are in our true nature. We are not separate.

Tenzin Palmo

Side view of Ryozen Kwannon | Kyoto, Japan
Sculptor Hirosuke Ishikawa completed this massive concrete sculpture of Guanyin in 1955 in commemoration of soldiers from every country killed in Japan in WWII. Eighty feet tall and weighing five hundred tons, it lies at the foot of an evergreen covered mountain range east of Kyoto. The Buddha on the top of her head is three feet tall. The same figure is on the cover of the book.

Tenzin Palmo, *Reflections on a Mountain Lake,* NY: Snow Lion Publications, 2002. Tenzin Palmo was given the rare title in Tibetan Buddhism of Jetsunma, Venerable Master. She completed over 12 years of solitary retreat in a cave in India and founded the Donggyo Gatsal Ling Nunnery where she bases her teaching.

Candle Attendant | Lungshan Temple, Taipei, Taiwan
Interacting with a practitioner, this woman reduces the fire hazard by attending to the lighted candles. People from all walks of life volunteer time or donate money to maintain the beauty of temple life. Lungshang Temple was originally devoted to Guanyin. Later, deities of the Taoist faith were added, reflecting the tolerance for religious diversity in Chinese traditions.

Chanting and Praying Together | Lungshan Temple, Manka, Taipei, Taiwan
Standing side by side, yet focused on their individual spiritual practice, these women and men reflect joy, devotion and concentration. They may be Taoist, Buddhist or both. Both faiths have influenced one another in their long intertwined history in China. Chan (Zen) Buddhism adopted from Taoism an emphasis on harmony with the natural world.

Cheng Yen, *Still Thoughts,* Volume Two, Taipei: Still Thoughts Cultural Publishing Co., Ltd., 1996. Buddhist nun, Master Cheng Yen, founded the Compassion Relief organization, Tzu Chi, based in Taiwan. With over 10 million volunteer members, it provides disaster relief and other significant service throughout the world.

To learn Buddha's character, you must maintain the attitude of impartiality. You must feel equally happy towards every person you meet. When you look at others through the eyes of Buddha, everyone will be a buddha.

Cheng Yen

Silence is the shaft we descend to the depths of contemplation. Silence is the vehicle that takes us to the innermost center of our being which is the place for all authentic practice.

Elaine MacInnes

Woman with Mala Beads | Jogyesa Temple, Seoul, Korea
Buddhist recitations are often in the form of an aspiration to awaken our capacity for compassion, wisdom and peace. Using mala beads to count each sacred word or phase, chants are recited to invoke our basic goodness or inherent Buddha Nature.

Elaine MacInnes, *"Elaine MacInnes" in Anne Bancroft, Women in Search of the Sacred*, London: Arkana, 1996. Sister MacInnes is an Irish Catholic nun who trained extensively in the Zen tradition in Japan. Her book, *Zen Contemplation for Christians,* integrates Zen meditation with Christian prayer.

As you see into every level of nature
pure and simple, things get deeper
and more profound. You know and let go,
know and let go, know and let go—*empty!*
Whatever appears, you let go. The important
principle in your gazing inward is simply to let go.

Upasika Kee Nanayon

"Fear Not" | Marble Mountain, Vietnam
Sitting at a cave altar, this earthy wooden sculpture speaks to the vernacular expression of Guanyin as the Female
Buddha. She solidly sits in meditation posture with one hand in the Fear Not or calm-abiding mudra and the other
hand resting in her lap in the meditation mudra. Next to her is a contemporary feminine rendition popular on personal
altars.

Upasika Kee Nanoyon, *Pure and Simple: Teachings of a Thai Buddhist Laywoman,* Boston: Wisdom Publications, 2005.
Upasika Kee, Thailand's foremost woman Buddhist teacher, started a meditation center that she led for 34 years until her
death in 1979. Teaching in the Thai Forest Tradition, she was known for her simplicity and directness.

Heaven is indeed a beautiful place but I will not enter it until I have united it with this world in which I live.

Houn Jiyu Kennett

But skillful meditation, that journey into the wilderness where we confront our own tricks and delusions, can empower social action, freeing us to respond in simplicity and immediacy to our fellow beings.

Joanna Macy

Kwannon and Maple Leaves | Western Kyoto cemetery, Japan
Bright green maple leaves provide a picturesque frame for this garden Kwannon in a temple cemetery. Experiencing the beauty of the landscape is an essential aspect of the Buddhist experience in Japan. Garden settings provide opportunities for quiet reflection and connection to the calming spirit of Kwannon.

Joanna Macy, *Mutual Causality in Buddhism and General Systems Theory: The Dharma of Natural Systems,* NY: State University of New York Press, 1991. Macy is a scholar of Buddhism, general systems theory and deep ecology. She is a long time spiritual activist in movements for peace, justice and ecology. She provides learning and service opportunities for others.

I think that the most beautiful and warm and comforting thing in the world is the selfless and compassionate smile a mother has for her child. The smile of a mother is that of the Buddha. Peace of mind and peace in the world will flow from a smile like that of a mother.

Chiko Komatsu

Nun, Woman and Child | Banyon, Ankor Wat, Cambodia

Despite their precarious status and meager resources, nuns in Cambodia dedicate their lives to assisting others in spiritual practice. I observed this cheerful nun make genuine contact with every passerby, offering incense and warmth no matter what the response. She offered this broad smile when I gestured to request a photograph.

Chiko Komatsu, *The Way to Peace: The Life and Teachings of the Buddha,* Kyoto: Hosakan Publishing Co., 1989. Chiko Komatsu was head of Jakkoin, a renowned monastery in Kyoto. At an early age she knew she wanted to become a nun and was ordained by age 11. In her later years she traveled worldwide working for peace.

Don't you know that afflictions are nothing more
	than wisdom?
And that the purest of blossoms emerges from
	the mire?

Benming

Women Praying to Guanyin │ Taipei, Taiwan
In 1997, this statue was erected in Taipei and was soon smeared with feces by a dissident Christian sect. Deeply concerned, activist Buddhist nun Reverend Chao Hwei went without food and water for six days at the site. A ground swell of community support grew around her and she succeeded in ensuring the continued placement of Guanyin in the park.

Benming, Beata Grant, *Daughters of Emptiness: Poems of Chinese Buddhist Nuns,* Somerville, MA: Wisdom Publications, 2003. Little is known about Benming, a nun of tenth century China who received a lineage transmission from a great Buddhist master of her time. Her poetry was published and quoted in sermons after her death by other Zen masters.

Dedicating Prayers with Incense | Quan Am Pagoda, Ho Chi Minh City, Vietnam
Three incense sticks are held at the forehead as a sign of dedication and represent the Buddha, Dharma and Sangha.
These three jewels signify the cornerstones of practice. The Buddha represents our capacity to awaken, the Dharma
represents truth we must embrace, and the Sangha is the community of practitioners who support and guide us on
the path.

Judith Simmer-Brown, *Dakini's Warm Breath: The Feminine Principle in Tibetan Buddhism,* Boston: Shambhala, 2001.
Acharya Simmer-Brown is a senior teacher in the Shambhala tradition and Professor of Buddhist and Religious Studies
at Naropa University in Boulder, Colorado. She is well known for her scholarship in inter-religious dialogue.

When purified of self-centeredness, passion is expressed as devotion to others, caring skillfully and utterly about their welfare; it is also expressed as joy in living and appreciation of the unique beauty of each moment.

May you be fearless.
May you make your life
breathtakingly beautiful
through your acts of generosity
and compassion.
May these same acts
make the world a cleaner
and safer place for the children
of our children.

Geri Larkin

Statue of Mother with Children | Bangkok, Thailand. Wandering into an unidentified Buddhist temple grounds under reconstruction, I discovered this delightful Chinese statue of a mother with one child in her arms and another clinging to her clothes. It tells a classic story of motherly love seen in art throughout the world.

Geri Larkin, *Plant Seed, Pull Weed: Nurturing the Garden of Your Life,* NY: HarperOne, 2008. P'arang Larkin trained in Korean Buddhism and founded Still Point Zen Temple in Detroit. Her sense of humor is evident in the titles of her many books including *The Chocolate Cake Sutra* and *Stumbling Toward Enlightenment.*

Once compassionate
vision is awakened, then
your strength, longing,
and inspiration increase
in unexpected ways.

Cynthia Kneen

Two Golden Bodhisattvas | Wat Pho, Bangkok, Thailand
In the courtyard of the oldest temple in Bangkok visitors adorn the statues of Guanyin with beaded necklaces. A woman was praying at this site early Christmas morning. The temple sponsored a grade school and we delighted in the voices of children playing with the music of Frosty the Snow Man in the background.

Many Arms of the Bodhisattva | Wat Pho, Bangkok, Thailand
Each hand of the bodhisattva Avelokitesvara holds a sacred implement or is in a gesture representing a skillful method to assist others. The implements include a lotus flower representing stainless wisdom, a rosary for making aspirations, a jewel symbolizing the enlightened mind, a vessel of healing balms and a sword to cut through to truth.

Cynthia Kneen, *Awake Mind, Open Heart: The Power of Courage and Dignity in Everyday Life*, NY: Marlowe & Company, 2002. Kneen teaches meditation and has written books in the Shambhala tradition of Vajrayana Buddhism. She is a management consultant and has taught mindfulness, leadership and effective business practices for 25 years.

Freedom is not just an end result. It is not something that awaits us at the end of our endeavor. Freedom is instantaneous, right now, from the very beginning. We can be "free" in the very process of the search, in experiencing, in every step along the way.

Thynn Thynn

Nun Studying for Exam | Samaidodaya Recluse, Sagaing, Myanmar
This nun is the attendant of the head abbess. While we visited with the elder abbess she studied for an exam she would take the next day at a Buddhist university. Her studies included English and she shared the challenging Buddhist philosophy she was to be tested on.

Thynn Thynn, *Living Meditation, Living Insight,* Mass: The Dhamma Dana Publication Fund, 1995. Thynn is a Chinese born retired physician and teacher of Insight Meditation in the Theravada tradition. Trained under Burmese masters, she is the resident teacher of the Sae Taw Winn II Dhamma Center in California.

You can't see wisdom, but you can see
its reflection. Its reflection is happiness,
fearlessness, and kindness.

Sylvia Boorstein

Women with Chant Books | Jogyesa Temple, Seoul, Korea
The Heart Sutra is a universal chant in Mahayana Buddhism and was recited when I visited the Jogyesa Temple. It is
written as a conversation between Avelokitesvara and Shariputra, a disciple of the Buddha. Avelokitasvara describes to
Shariputra the experience of awakening to the wisdom of emptiness while engaged in meditation.

Sylvia Boorstein, *It's Easier Than You Think,* Harper: San Francisco, 1995.
Boorstein, of the Vipassana tradition, co-founded Spirit Rock Meditation Center in California and teaches throughout
the United States. She demystifies spirituality with stories of the everyday infused with wisdom.

If we human beings do not understand ourselves freely, profoundly, from moment to moment, there cannot be any intelligent, loving, and compassionate relationship among us. Division and sorrow will persist. Is that clear?

Toni Packer

Kwannon in Temple Garden | Eikan-do Temple, Kyoto, Japan
This tall garden Kwannon holds a vase of flowers and is depicted as wearing ornate jewelry and robes. The eleven faces on her crown and surrounding her head represent her far-reaching vision. A serene corner of a Japanese temple garden is often set aside for her elegant figure.

Toni Packer, *The Work of This Moment,* Boston: Shambhala, 2007.
Packer is the founder and head of the Springwater Center for Meditative Inquiry and Retreats where she emphasizes looking beyond all forms including the rituals and concepts of her original Zen training.

When we have an intuitive understanding of our inner goodness, self-acceptance is natural. The more we practice, the more we will have tastes of our inner goodness, until we come to celebrate ourselves fully.

Diana Winston

Royal Ease Posture | Water Beauty Art Street, Sanyi, Taiwan

This bronze sculpture captures the essence of complete relaxation within realization. Her body posture is open yet dignified, assured yet appreciative. In her manifestation as royalty, Guanyin emanates command and far reaching influence. Her foot extending toward the ground represents her readiness to step into the world to assist others as needed.

Diana Winston, *Wide Awake: A Buddhist Guide for Teens,* NY: Perigee Trade, 2003. Winston is a Vipassana teacher and Director of Mindfulness Education at UCLA's Mindful Awareness Research Center. She practiced as a Buddhist nun for a year in Burma and teaches meditation to youth and adults.

Appreciating one's life generates a
courageous heart and a courageous mind.

Khandro Rinpoche

Girl Praying | Prohm, Ankor Wat, Cambodia
This young girl spends her day accompanying an elder nun who offers blessings to visitors at the ruins of Ankor Wat.
Over the course of Cambodia's early history of war with Muslims, many of the Buddhist statues were beheaded.
Nevertheless, nuns carefully tend these statues creating sacred space with altars of burning incense.

Khandro Rinpoche, *This Precious Life,* Boston: Shambhala, 2003.
Khandro is a fully empowered teacher from the Mindrolling lineage of the Nyingma tradition. Her lineage has a history
of great female masters since the 17th century. She leads many Buddhist centers and teaches worldwide.

Figure with Branch | Wat Arun, Bangkok, Thailand
Wat Arun, one of the oldest Buddhist temples in Bangkok, has a lovely entrance courtyard with numerous Chinese statues of women holding symbolic offerings. This elegant lady holds a branch with spring blossoms. While Buddhist statuary made in Thailand is singularly male, Chinese immigrants introduced female imagery at numerous temple sites.

Figure with Offering | Wat Arun, Bangkok, Thailand
This figure is holding an offering, a symbol of gratitude and an opportunity for contemplation. Generosity is the first of the six Paramitas in Buddhism, traits to be cultivated on the path to liberation. The Paramita of generosity includes charitable giving and also refers to the unconditional love of an open heart and mind.

Joan Halifax, *Being With Dying: Cultivating Compassion and Fearlessness in the Presence of Death.* Boston: Shambhala, 2008. Roshi Halifax is founder and abbot of the Upaya Zen Center in New Mexico. She is the Director of the Project on Being with Dying and the Upaya Prison Project. She was an Honorary Research Fellow at Harvard University.

So recognize your limits with compassion; share your joy, stability, strength, openness, and humor; help to create a strong, supportive community; and above all, don't neglect the practice of self-care. If you really want to take care of the whole world, start by taking care of your life.

Joan Halifax

Perfectly aware,
Not a thought,
Just the moon
Piercing me with light
As I gaze upon it.

Otagaki Rengetsu

Water Moon Guanyin | Water Beauty Art Street, Sanyi, Taiwan
The moon's reflection in the water is a common metaphor for "emptiness" and the illusory nature of all dharmas, or truth. To realize the truth of emptiness is to understand the impermanent nature of all things. This teaching, associated with the Water-moon Guanyin, liberates humans from clinging to the illusion of self and the suffering it causes.

Otagaki Rengetsu, John Stevens, trans., *Lotus Moon: The Poetry of Rengetsu,* White Pine Press, 2005. Rengetsu, a Buddhist nun in 19th century Japan, is regarded as one of the great poets of her time. After the loss of three infant children and two husbands she found meaning in her life of service as a renunciate and artist.

I pay homage to you, mind itself:
primordial lucid clarity by nature,
satisfying all needs and desires,
like a wish-fulfilling jewel.

Niguma

Guanyin and Dragon | Wat Indravihan, Bangkok, Thailand
Guanyin is often associated with a dragon, a symbol in Asia of auspicious power and potency. The juxtaposition of the two depicts her equanimity as equal to the dragon's formidable strength. The roar of the dragon is said to be compassionate thunder to awaken us from delusion. Protective dragons are often placed near spiritual figures at temple sites.

Niguma, Harding, Sarah. *Niguma, Lady of Illusion,* Ithaca: NY: Snow Lion Publications, 2010. Niguma is a renowned eleventh-century woman and founder of tantric practices in one of the great Tibetan lineages of spiritual masters. Her realization is evidenced in the texts of her teaching recently translated by Lama Harding.

Spiritual practice means having faith that there is a great treasure within your mind, and then finding it. Learning to discover the treasure within you is the most worthwhile thing in the world. If you can put this into practice, you can live freshly, with a mind open like the sky, always overflowing with compassion. What could be better than this?

Daehaeng Sunim

Dharma Drum Guanyin | Dharma Drum Center, Jinshan, Taiwan
This eight-foot-tall bronze statue, *Welcoming Guanyin,* greets visitors at the entrance to the Dharma Drum Center, a large Buddhist compound containing a monastery, university, large practice halls and spacious grounds in the rolling hills of northern Taiwan. Standing on a lotus flower, her flowing robes catch the breeze and her crown reaches to the heavens.

Daehaeng Sunim, "Who is Healing?" Bachelor, Martine, *Walking on Lotus Flowers,* London: Thorsons, 1996. Daehaeng Sunim is a revered teacher in Korea who practiced in solitude for over 12 years in the wilderness. Unusual in her tradition, her many students include monks. She has a recent illuminating book, *No River to Cross.*

Vesak at Jogyesa Temple | Jogyesa Temple, Seoul, Korea
Hundreds of practitioners gather to chant and offer prostrations in honor of Vesak during the yearly celebration of the Buddha's birth, enlightenment and passing at death into Nirvana. A very old Bodhi tree stands outside this temple and is surrounded by thousands of hanging paper lanterns. The Buddha gained enlightenment sitting beneath a Bodhi tree.

Three Women in Prayer | Jogyesa Temple, Seoul, Korea
My clicking camera did not deter the concentration of these women as they made silent prayers during the morning Vesak service. Prayers are often in the form of recitations of Buddhist teachings, sacred syllables or the names of the bodhisattvas, particularly Guanyin.

Dipa Ma, "Everyday Dharma," in Michelle Levey, Karma Kekshe Tsomo, ed., *Buddhism Through American Women's Eyes,* Ithaca, NY: Snow Lion Publications, 1995. Dipa Ma, known as "the patron saint of householders," exemplified an integrated life of mindfulness and mothering. Born in Bangladesh and trained under a Burmese master, she blessed those who sought her profound peace.

My mind has three qualities: concentration, equanimity, and loving kindness. That's it.

Dipa Ma

The mind is not enslaved by joy or misery,
Nor caught in apathy. But patient,
It withstands both good and ill:
This is Tsogyal's patience—
Tibetan Yeshe Tsogyal.

Yeshe Tsogyal

Tara Mandala Retreat Center | Pagosa Springs, Colorado, USA
When the aspiration to achieve enlightenment arose in Tara she was urged to pray to be reborn as a man so she could become a Buddha. She ignored the advice and vowed to remain in a woman's body and work for the benefit of others until everyone was released from suffering. Trust in her essential Buddha Nature allowed her to throw off social convention.

Yeshe Tsogyal, Gyalwa Changchub and Namkhai Nyingpo, trans., *Lady of the Lotus-Born: The Life and Enlightenment of Yeshe Tsogyal*, Shambhala: Boston & London: 1999. Yeshe Tsogyal is considered the mother of Tibetan Vajrayana Buddhism and a dakini, symbol of the feminine principle. She was a queen in 8th century Tibet and became an accomplished practitioner renowned for her realization.

Get rid of the tendency to judge yourself above, below, or equal to others. By penetrating deeply into judgment you will live at peace.

Abhirupa-Nanda

Guanyin Being Carved | Water Beauty Art Street, Sanyi, Taiwan
The sculptor's tools lay next to Guanyin coming into being. She expresses a work in progress, something we can imagine ourselves to be as we progress along the path. She begs us to ask the questions: Am I shaping my hands to serve others? Do my robes enfold me in serenity? Is Buddha Nature resting in the forefront of my mind?

Wood Carved Guanyins | Water Beauty Art Street, Sanyi, Taiwan
The reiterating pattern of these statues is a reminder that we receive the blessings of the many living bodhisattvas manifest in the world. She is not a single figure but a potential within the heart of every human being. Each heart exists within a community of practitioners encouraging us on the path of awakening.

Abhirupa-Nanda, Susan Murcott, *The First Buddhist Women: Translations and Commentary on the Therigatha*, Berkeley: Parallax Press, 1991. Abhirupa-Nanda was a Buddhist nun in India at the time of the Buddha. Her poems are recorded in the Therigatha, a collection of enlightenment poems by women who directly encountered the Buddha.

Be tough. But be tough the way a blade of grass is: rooted, willing to lean, and at peace with what's around it.

Natalie Goldberg

Garden Statue with Leaves | Wat Pho, Bangkok, Thailand
Numerous formed concrete statues from China were added to Buddhist sites in Thailand at the turn of the century. This graceful figure reflects the emphasis on symmetry with nature often found in feminine statuary in Asian art. Harmony is considered a fundamental value and is expressed through Chan (Zen) Buddhist teachings that originated in China.

Natalie Goldberg, *Wild Mind: Living the Writer's Life,* NY: Quality Paperback Book Club, 1991. Goldberg, Zen practitioner and best selling author of *Writing Down the Bones,* teaches writing as an awareness practice. Sharing her own trials and breakthrough moments, she invites readers to trust their experience.

I still recall, how with my bag on a pole,
    I forgot my yesterdays,
Wandering the hills, played in the waters,
    went to the land of the clouds.
The lift of an eyebrow, the blink of an eye--
    all of it is samadhi;
In this great world there is nowhere that is
    not a wisdom hall.

Ziyong

Jizo and Kwannon | Western Kyoto cemetery, Japan
The bodhisattvas, Jizo and Kwannon, are often placed together in cemeteries. Jizo is supplicated in ceremonies for children who have died, including those who have been aborted. Statues of Jizo are ubiquitous throughout Japan, as families will offer a statue of him at sites for their deceased family member, child or loved one who has suffered.

Ziyong, Beata Grant, *Daughters of Emptiness: Poems of Chinese Buddhist Nuns,* Boston: Wisdom Publications, 2003. Ziyong lived the life of a renunciate in 18th century China. Receiving Dharma transmission after several decades of Buddhist study and practice, she was the abbess of numerous convents with many devoted students.

...there is no single savior
being awaited. Rather,
the savior is spread out
among us, emerging from
each of us as we bring
the fruits from our sacred
garden into our daily lives.
It is we who must save us.

Patricia Hopkins &
Sherry Ruth Anderson

Flower Market Artisan and Lotus Bud Bouquets | Flower Market, Bangkok, Thailand Lotus.
Flowers for Buddhist altars and ceremonies surround this elder Thai woman. She is encircled by other women selling their handicraft as she creates bouquets on the sidewalk of the central flower market in Bangkok. I was struck by her grace and dignity amid the bustle of the marketplace.

Patricia Hopkins & Sherry Ruth Anderson. *The Feminine Face of God: The Unfolding of the Sacred in Women,* NY: Bantam Books, 1991. Hopkins and Anderson broke ground with their seminal and best selling book, *The Feminine Face of God.* They interviewed female leaders of many faiths in search of cogent and inspiring themes in women's spirituality.

Sit like a mountain. Sit with a sense of strength and dignity. Be steadfast, be majestic, be natural and at ease in awareness. No matter how many winds are blowing, no matter how many clouds are swirling, no matter how many lions are prowling, be intimate with everything, and sit like a mountain.

Sharon Salzberg

Sitting on a Lion | Marble Mountain, Vietnam. Outside the Marble Mountain caves many large sculptures of Guanyin stand along the roadside, commissioned by temples or waiting for potential buyers. This fifteen-foot sculpture shows her in the royal ease posture, calmly sitting on the back of a ferocious lion, confident and at one with all of life.

Sharon Salzberg, *The Kindness Handbook,* Boulder, CO: Sounds True, Inc., 2008. Salzberg trained in the Theravada tradition and is known for her teaching on insight meditation and loving-kindness. She co-founded the Insight Meditation Society, the Barre Center for Buddhist Studies and the Forest Refuge retreat center.

Punna, be filled with all good things
like the moon on the fifteenth day.
Completely, perfectly full
of wisdom
tear open
the massive dark.

Punna

Guanyin Paper Lantern Float | Lotus Lantern Parade, Seoul, Korea
Approximately twenty feet tall, this Guanyin figure stood out among a series of male figures significant in the Buddhist pantheon. It wasn't until I looked more closely at the photograph that I noticed the mustache painted on her face. This is an unusual addition for a Guanyin figure wearing a veil, as this type of head covering indicates a feminine depiction.

Punna, Susan Murcott, *The First Buddhist Women: Translations and Commentary on the Therigatha,* Berkeley: Parallax Press, 1991. We know little of Punna, a nun in the time of the Buddha, other than at age twenty she joined the sangha of nuns under the leadership of Mahapajapati. She was among 500, a number representing "a great many", who formed the women's community.

Awakening warriors understand that there are no enemies. Everyone belongs and has a right to happiness and living a life free of oppression and unnecessary suffering. We leave no one behind. Each of us goes forth in our own lives of enlightened being with the full and complete intention of bringing every single soul with us.

Angel Kyodo Williams

Marching Band and Nun Playing Cymbals | Lotus Lantern Parade, Seoul, Korea
The resounding clap of cymbals punctuated the parade, reminding everyone to wake up to the freshness of the moment. The bell, drum, gong and clappers are used in Buddhist ceremonies to focus attention and elicit appreciation for the moment. This lively group of nuns and monks marched and played their instruments with precision and joy.

Angel Kyodo Williams, *Being Black: Zen and the Art of Living with Fearlessness and Grace,* NY: Viking Compass, 2000. Williams is a Zen priest, spiritual director of the New Dharma Meditation Community and founder of the Center for Transformative Change. As teacher, activist and artist, she addresses issues of race and social change.

Acknowledgements

I owe tremendous appreciation to friends and colleagues who have contributed to this book with the warmth of companionship, cogent insight, feminist viewpoints, fine-tuned editing, and faith in the substance of the book.

Judith Simmer Brown was a guiding light, precise Buddhist editor, and crucial to my own confidence in the important contributions of *The Female Buddha*. Patricia Hopkins lent her spiritual strength and sharp aesthetic vision to the editing of both the writing and compilation of images.

My 18-year-long companions in the "Writers Group," Linda Leonard and Betty Cannon, shared their passion, insight and uplifting support to the end. Reverend Jenkir Shih became an immediate friend and cross-cultural guide to the world of Guanyin and Buddhism in Taiwan. Kelly Lin Lee generously provided a serene refuge in Taipei.

My husband, Stephen Burden, is central to this list, often contributing spur of the moment ideas as well as keen Buddhist and artistic critique, while doing double duty in sustaining affection and good cheer during the years I was glued to the computer.

My teacher, Dzogchen Ponlop Rinpoche, kindled the "Rebel Heart of the Female Buddha" at just the right moment during my work on this book. I am indebted to his vision of a genuine Western Buddhism free of cultural hang-ups.

Deb Piranian and Polly Mahoney were constant friends, most often sharing their support as we walked the foothills of the Rockies. The women of my ongoing Nonviolent Communication group offered strategic support as I wrestled with my inner demons. The Nalandabodhi Boulder sangha was unconditional in their friendship.

Tara Mandala Retreat Center in Pagosa Springs kindly offered me a "photographer's retreat" and Naropa University provided a grant for a portion of the overseas research. Venerable Dhammananda was a generous host at the Songdhammakalyani Monastery in Thailand. With delight, Jonathan X. Lee shared his scholarship on Guanyin and Mazu.

Julie Trelstad, owner of JulieInk and Booktiq, offered critical guidance in the process of design and publishing. Jim Gritz coached me in photography and lent his artistic eye. Monika Edgar created the exquisite layout and Joanne Bolton guided me through the maze of printing a fine arts book.

Many others, too numerous to name, offered rich conversation and much needed assistance with the project. The kindness of strangers enriched my overseas journey and opened my heart to the love Guanyin engenders throughout the world.

Girl in Buddha Pose | Lotus Lantern Festival, Seoul, Korea